FAMILY

DEVOTIONAL

FOR PARENTS

AND KIDS

Published by Midsummer Bloom Books

First Edition: September 2025
Printed in the United States of America.

Contents

Introduction

Welcome to The 52-Week Family Devotional for Parents and Kids. This book is a weekly rhythm of Scripture, story, conversation, and activity designed to help your family grow closer to God and each other. You don't need to be Bible experts or have hours of free time. You just need a few moments each week, open hearts, and a willingness to listen, laugh, and learn together.

Each week includes:

* A theme verse from the ESV Bible to anchor your hearts.

* A short opening thought to set the tone.

* An original family story that connects the Bible's truth to everyday life.

* Discussion questions to spark meaningful conversations.

* A creative family activity that brings the theme to life.

* A simple prayer to close.

You can read these around the dinner table, on a Sunday afternoon, or before bedtime. Some weeks will feel easy, others might touch tender places. That's okay. God meets us right where we are. Pray before you begin, invite everyone to share, and let grace set the tone.

Families grow stronger one faithful step at a time. Let's take those steps together.

Week 1: God's Word Lights Our Path

"Your word is a lamp to my feet and a light to my path." — Psalm 119:105 (ESV)

OPENING THOUGHT

Have you ever tried to walk through a dark room without a light? You bump into things you couldn't see. God's Word is like a lamp, helping us see what's true, good, and wise—right where our feet are, and where to step next.

FAMILY STORY

On Sunday night, the Wilsons decided to try a new family tradition: "Tech-Free Trek." They would take an evening walk without phones and see what they noticed. Ten minutes in, the sun slipped behind the trees and the path through the park turned dim. "I can't see the rocks," Emma whispered, gripping Dad's hand.

Dad pulled a small flashlight from his pocket. "I brought this just in case." The beam cut through the shadows, showing roots that would have tripped them and a little puddle waiting to soak their socks. As they walked, Noah asked, "Why not bring a giant spotlight to light the whole park?"

Mom smiled. "Sometimes God gives us enough light for the next step. His Word works like that. We might not see the entire year ahead, but He shows us how to live today."

Back home, Emma opened her Bible and read a verse about kindness. That week, when a classmate forgot her lunch, Emma remembered the "lamp" and quietly shared half of hers.

It didn't solve all the problems at school, but it lit up that moment. And that's how the Wilsons began looking for little lights in every day.

DISCUSSION QUESTIONS

1. When have you felt unsure about what to do next? What "light" did God give you?

2. What is one area of life where you need God's guidance right now?

3. How can we make space this week to let God's Word be our "lamp"?

FAMILY ACTIVITY: VERSE-PATH LANTERNS

Create simple "lanterns" by wrapping a strip of paper around a clear jar. Each person writes a short verse on the paper (like Psalm 119:105) and decorates it with stars or footprints. Tape the paper to fit, place a battery tea light inside, and turn off the lights. Talk about how a small truth can guide a big decision. Keep the lanterns on the dinner table this week; when they're lit, read your verse aloud and share one "next step" you'll take with God's help.

PRAYER

Lord, thank You for Your Word that lights our path. Help us trust the light You give today and follow where You lead tomorrow. In Jesus' name, Amen.

Week 2: Unfailing Love

"Love never ends." — 1 Corinthians 13:8 (ESV)

OPENING THOUGHT

Feelings can come and go like weather, but God's love isn't like that. His love is steady, strong, and always at work—even when we mess up or feel far away.

FAMILY STORY

The Martinez family had a Friday tradition: "Taco and Tell." Everyone shared a win and a wobble from their week. This Friday, Leo's wobble spilled out in tears. He had lost his temper and yelled at his little sister, Maya, when she borrowed his markers without asking. He felt terrible, but the words were already out.

Mom reached over and squeezed Leo's hand. "Thank you for being honest." Maya nodded from across the table. "I shouldn't have taken your markers," she whispered. The room felt heavy.

Dad took a deep breath. "You know, God's love doesn't end when we fail. It stays. It teaches. It helps us try again." He turned to Maya. "And love helps us respect each other's things."

They decided to make a "Borrow Box" for shared items. If someone needed something that wasn't theirs, they'd put a note in the box. By Sunday, Leo found a note from Maya asking to use his markers for a card she wanted to make him. He smiled and wrote, "Yes—please!" The card said, "I'm sorry.

I love you." Their week held mistakes and mending, but the thread running through was love that didn't give up.

DISCUSSION QUESTIONS

1. When have you worried that love might run out? What helped you feel secure again?

2. How does God's unfailing love change how we forgive or ask forgiveness?

3. What can our family do to show love that lasts even on hard days?

FAMILY ACTIVITY: THE UNENDING HEART

Cut a long strip of paper for each person. On the strip, write ways your family shows love (listening, apologizing, serving). Tape the ends to form a loop. Link each loop to make a chain and hang it where everyone can see. Add a new loop each time someone practices one of the words this week. Watch the "love chain" grow as a reminder that love keeps going.

PRAYER

Father, thank You that Your love never ends. Teach us to love each other with patience and forgiveness, just like You love us. In Jesus' name, Amen.

Week 3: Talking with God

"pray without ceasing" — 1 Thessalonians 5:17
(ESV)

OPENING THOUGHT

Prayer isn't a fancy speech. It's a conversation with God that can happen in the car, at the table, or on the playground. God welcomes our whispers, our worries, and our thank-yous.

FAMILY STORY

On the way to school, the Patel minivan sounded like a popcorn machine—popping with questions. "Did I put my homework in my backpack?" "Will I make the team?" "Is it going to rain?" Mom smiled in the rearview mirror. "Let's pop those questions into prayer."

Eight-year-old Priya frowned. "Do we have to close our eyes?" Dad laughed. "Not while driving." He showed them "thread prayers"—one-sentence prayers stitched through the day. "Thank You for this sunrise." "Help me be brave in math." "Give me kind words."

That afternoon, Priya bumped knees with a classmate while going for the same book. Her classmate snapped, "Watch it!" Priya felt heat rise in her cheeks. She remembered the thread prayers and breathed, "Jesus, help me respond kindly." She said, "I'm sorry. Are you okay?" The tension melted.

At bedtime, the family shared their thread prayers. Some were tiny, like "Thanks for extra fries." Some were deep, like "Please heal Mr. Nguyen." Mom said, "God hears them all." Priya grinned. "It's like sending texts to God—and He never turns off notifications." Everyone laughed, and they ended the day with one more thread: "Thank You for listening, God."

DISCUSSION QUESTIONS

1. When do you find it easiest to talk to God? When is it hardest?

2. What is one-sentence prayer you can pray tomorrow?

3. How can our family remind each other to pray throughout the day?

FAMILY ACTIVITY: PRAYER THREADS

Give each person a piece of string or yarn and tie it loosely around a wrist or place it in a pocket. Each time you notice it, pause for a one-sentence prayer. At dinner, place the strings in a bowl and share a favorite "thread" from the day. Keep the bowl on the table this week to remember that prayer weaves through everything.

PRAYER

God, thank You for always listening. Teach us to talk with You throughout our day and to listen for Your gentle leading. In Jesus' name, Amen.

Week 4: Courage for the Next Step

"Be strong and courageous." — Joshua 1:9 (ESV)

OPENING THOUGHT

Courage doesn't mean we're never afraid—it means we trust God enough to move forward anyway. He goes with us into new schools, hard talks, and uncertain moments.

FAMILY STORY

When the school musical announced auditions, Mateo's stomach turned inside out. He loved singing in his room but dreaded singing in front of strangers. His older sister, Lila, remembered her own shaky first audition. "Let's practice together," she said, handing him a hairbrush as a pretend microphone.

They practiced in the living room while Mom chopped veggies and Dad clapped along. On audition day, Mateo's hands trembled. As he stood in the hallway, he spotted a note tucked into his backpack: "Be strong and courageous. We believe in you. — Lila."

Inside the audition room, the pianist nodded, and the music began. Mateo's voice squeaked on the first note. He bit his lip, looked down, and whispered a prayer: "God, help." The next line came smoother. Then stronger. When he finished, he felt lighter, like he'd carried a heavy backpack up a hill and set it down.

He didn't land the lead role, but he got a part and made two new friends at rehearsal. At dinner that night, Mateo said, "Being brave wasn't about being perfect. It was singing the next note." Dad smiled. "And God met you right there, on that note."

DISCUSSION QUESTIONS

1. What's something coming up that feels scary? What's one "next note" you can take?

2. How have you seen God help you be brave before?

3. How can we support each other when we need courage?

FAMILY ACTIVITY: COURAGE CARDS

Cut small cards. On one side, write a brave step each person faces this week (a test, a conversation, a tryout). On the other side, write the theme verse. Trade cards so each person prays for someone else's step. Keep the cards visible—on a mirror or lunchbox. Share "God showed up" moments at the week's end.

PRAYER

God, when we feel afraid, remind us You are with us. Give us strength to take the next step and courage to keep going. In Jesus' name, Amen.

Week 5: Forgive and Be Free

"forgive, and you will be forgiven;" — Luke 6:37 (ESV)

OPENING THOUGHT

Forgiveness doesn't say, "It didn't matter." It says, "I won't carry this hurt forever." God forgives us, and He helps us forgive others so our hearts can heal.

FAMILY STORY

During a backyard soccer game, Tessa slid for the ball and accidentally kicked her cousin Eli's shin. Eli yelped and stormed off, slamming the screen door. Tessa's stomach sank. "It was an accident," she muttered, but the guilt stuck.

Later, Eli's shin wore a purple mark and his pride wore a bruise. At dinner, conversation dripped like a leaky faucet—slow and tense. Grandpa finally spoke. "In our family, we say what was wrong and we forgive."

Tessa looked at Eli. "I'm sorry I hurt you. I should have been more careful." Eli crossed his arms. Before he could answer, Grandma added, "Forgiveness is a gift we've all received. We don't hoard gifts—we share them."

Eli sighed. "I forgive you." The room exhaled. Grandpa stood up and stuck out his leg dramatically. "Back in my day, we invented shin guards out of couch cushions." Laughter bubbled up, and soon they were strapping dish towels to their shins and inventing goofy safety gear.

The bruise didn't disappear, but the bitterness did. Forgiveness didn't rewind the slide tackle; it rewired their hearts to love again.

DISCUSSION QUESTIONS

1. What makes it hard to forgive? What makes it easier?

2. When have you needed someone to forgive you? How did it feel?

3. Is there anyone you need to forgive—or ask forgiveness from—this week?

FAMILY ACTIVITY: THE STONE AND THE CROSS

Give each person a small stone. Think of a hurt you're carrying. Hold the stone tight, then place it at the base of a simple cross you make from two sticks or taped pencils. Pray for the person involved and ask God for grace to forgive. Leave the stones there for the week as a sign you're not carrying them alone.

Safety note: If you have very young children, use larger, lightweight objects (like foam balls) instead of small stones, and supervise closely to avoid choking hazards.

PRAYER

Merciful God, thank You for forgiving us. Help us release hurts and forgive others as You have forgiven us. In Jesus' name, Amen.

Week 6: Everyday Kindness

"Be kind to one another" — Ephesians 4:32 (ESV)

OPENING THOUGHT

Kindness is love wearing work boots. It shows up in small ways—holding a door, sharing a snack, or speaking gently. God's kindness to us overflows to others.

FAMILY STORY

The Nguyen family made a game of spotting kindness. They called it "Kind Catches." Each time someone saw or received kindness, they'd shout, "Caught one!" and drop a paper heart in a jar. The first day, the jar felt empty. By Wednesday, it clinked with stories.

At recess, Jonah saw a new kid, Mateo, standing alone by the swings. Jonah's stomach fluttered—what if Mateo didn't want to play? He remembered the jar and walked over. "Want to join our game?" Mateo's face brightened. "Sure!" After school, Jonah sounded the family alarm: "Caught one!" and wrote "invited Mateo" on a heart.

That evening, Mom found an anonymous bag of groceries on their porch with a note: "Just because. —A friend." She didn't know who left it, but she knew how it felt: seen. "Caught one," she whispered, dropping a heart in the jar.

By Saturday, the jar was full, not because they invented kindness, but because they began seeing it. Kindness didn't always look big; sometimes it looked like setting the table without being asked or laughing at someone's joke on a hard day.

DISCUSSION QUESTIONS

1. What's a small act of kindness that meant a lot to you?

2. Who might need kindness at school, work, or in our neighborhood this week?

3. How can we be kind when we don't feel like it?

FAMILY ACTIVITY: KINDNESS BINGO

Create a simple 3x3 bingo card with acts of kindness (write a thank-you note, sit with someone new, help with chores, encourage a teammate, pray for a friend, share a snack, pick up litter, send a text to a grandparent, say "please/thank you"). As a family, try to complete a "bingo" this week. Celebrate with a simple treat and share stories behind each square.

PRAYER

Lord, You have been so kind to us. Make our eyes quick to notice needs and our hands ready to help. In Jesus' name, Amen.

Week 7: Patient Hearts

"Love is patient and kind;" — 1 Corinthians 13:4
(ESV)

OPENING THOUGHT

Patience is love that takes a deep breath. It waits, listens, and trusts God's timing—even in long lines, slow Wi-Fi, or seasons that feel stuck.

FAMILY STORY

Saturday mornings were pancake mornings at the Harris house. This Saturday, the batter was lumpy, the griddle was slow to heat, and everyone was HUNGRY. Oliver hovered with a plate like a hummingbird, while Ava tapped the table with a fork drumroll.

Dad flipped one pancake and burned the next. "Why is this taking forever?" Oliver groaned. Mom laughed. "Because patience is on the menu." She set a timer for two minutes. "Let's try a patience challenge."

For two minutes, everyone named something good about waiting. Ava said, "You can smell the pancakes longer." Oliver said, "You can talk more." Dad said, "You can learn from the burned ones." When the timer beeped, they cheered as if it were a game.

Later that day, patience got tested again when the soccer game was delayed. Oliver, who usually fumed, surprised himself by starting a silly rhyming game with teammates to pass the time. By evening, as they ate the last stack of golden pancakes for dessert, Mom said, "We didn't speed up time, but patience changed us while we waited." Everyone agreed—

the pancakes tasted better because they were seasoned with grace.

DISCUSSION QUESTIONS

1. What makes waiting hard for you? What helps?

2. Where do you think God is asking our family to practice patience right now?

3. How can patience show love to others?

FAMILY ACTIVITY: THE PATIENCE PLANT

Plant fast-sprouting seeds (beans or herbs) in a small pot. Label it "Patience." Each day, water it and note small changes—sprouts, new leaves. When frustration pops up this week, glance at the plant and remember that growth takes time. When it finally sprouts, celebrate with a special meal where everyone shares a "slow-growing" area God is tending.

PRAYER

God, thank You for being patient with us. Grow patient hearts in our family as we trust Your timing. In Jesus' name, Amen.

Week 8: Gratitude Every Day

"Oh give thanks to the LORD, for he is good;" —
Psalm 107:1 (ESV)

OPENING THOUGHT

Gratitude is a habit that helps us notice God's gifts. When we say "thank You," we tune our hearts to His goodness—even on ordinary Mondays.

FAMILY STORY

The Alvarezes started a "Thankful Trail" on their hallway wall. Each night, they taped up paper leaves with something they were grateful for. The first week was easy: pizza night, a sunny day, a new book. The second week, a flat tire changed the mood.

Dad discovered the flat right before church. Everyone piled into Mom's car, crowded and grumpy. After service, a neighbor named Ms. Carol waved them over. "I saw your tire and brought my pump and patch kit," she said. Twenty minutes later, they were back in business.

That night, the Thankful Trail felt quieter. "Should we put up a leaf?" Maya asked. "The day was kind of rough." Mom nodded. "Maybe those are the most important leaves." They wrote, "Ms. Carol," "family teamwork," and "banana bread she gave us."

As the weeks went on, the trail twisted down the hall, full of big and small gratitude—good health reports and the smell of rain, a new friendship and a funny dog video. They realized that thankfulness wasn't pretending hard things weren't hard; it was seeing God's goodness nearby.

DISCUSSION QUESTIONS

1. What is one simple thing you're thankful for today?

2. How does gratitude change the way we feel and act?

3. How can we practice gratitude when a day is tough?

FAMILY ACTIVITY: GRATITUDE WALK

Take a 15-minute walk together. Each person shares three thanks: one you can see (like trees), one you can't see (like forgiveness), and one about a person. Snap or sketch simple "gratitude snapshots" along the way. Back home, post them where you'll see them. This week, add one new snapshot each day and say, "God, You are good."

PRAYER

Good Father, thank You for Your goodness in every season. Open our eyes to Your gifts and fill our mouths with thanks. In Jesus' name, Amen.

Week 9: Serving Like Jesus

"For even the Son of Man came not to be served
but to serve" — Mark 10:45 (ESV)

OPENING THOUGHT

Jesus didn't come to be the VIP; He came to wash feet, feed the hungry, and welcome the overlooked. When we serve, we look like Him.

FAMILY STORY

When their church announced a Saturday service day, the Cooper family signed up to clean up a local park. Liam grumbled. "Couldn't we do something more exciting?" Mom handed him a trash grabber. "Let's see what happens."

At first, it felt like chores. But soon, they met a dad tossing a ball with his toddler. "Thanks for making this place nice," he said, smiling shyly. They found a lost library book and returned it to a grateful librarian. They cleared a bench so an elderly couple could sit and watch the ducks.

As they ate sandwiches under a tree, Liam noticed a little girl trying to reach the monkey bars. He walked over. "Want a boost?" She nodded. He lifted her to the first rung, and her mom's eyes filled with tears. "She's been trying all week." Liam felt something warm bloom in his chest.

On the drive home, Liam admitted, "It wasn't exciting at first. Then it was better than exciting." Dad nodded. "Serving is like that. It starts with showing up. Then God shows you hearts."

DISCUSSION QUESTIONS

1. What holds us back from serving others? What helps us start?

2. Who around us could use help this week—at school, work, church, or home?

3. How does serving change the way we see people?

FAMILY ACTIVITY: SECRET SERVICE

Give each family member a "service mission" card with a specific, secret task (wash someone's dish, leave a kind note, take out trash, tidy shoes). Complete your mission without being caught. At week's end, reveal missions and tell the stories. Talk about how it felt to serve quietly, like Jesus.

PRAYER

Jesus, thank You for serving us. Make us ready to notice needs and joyful to help, even when no one sees. In Your name, Amen.

Week 10: Honest and True

"Lying lips are an abomination to the LORD" —
Proverbs 12:22 (ESV)

OPENING THOUGHT

Honesty builds trust like bricks build a strong house. Lies might feel like shortcuts, but they crack the foundation. God delights in truth.

FAMILY STORY

Riley loved art class, especially the monthly contest for the "Gallery Wall." This month, her painting of a red fox looked almost alive. She wanted to win so badly that when she noticed a tiny smudge near the eye, she grabbed a fine-tip marker to fix it—after the deadline. The rules were clear: no changes after submission.

Her heart pounded. "It's just a dot," she told herself. On Friday, she won. Everyone clapped. But inside, the victory felt hollow, like winning a race with a head start no one saw.

That night, Riley stared at the ceiling. She thought about God loving truth and the way her teacher trusted her. At breakfast, she swallowed hard. "I broke the rules. I fixed my painting after the deadline." The room went quiet. Dad squeezed her shoulder. "That was brave."

At school, Riley told her teacher. The teacher's eyes softened. "Thank you for your honesty. It matters more than a ribbon." They gave the prize to second place, and Riley helped hang the winning art. She didn't bring home a ribbon, but she carried something better: a lighter heart and a stronger trust.

DISCUSSION QUESTIONS

1. Why might someone be tempted to lie? What usually happens next?

2. When have you seen honesty repair trust?

3. What can our family do to make telling the truth safe and valued?

FAMILY ACTIVITY: TRUST TOWER

Use blocks or household items to build a tower. Each block represents truth-telling. For each real-life example of honesty from the week, add a block. If someone tells a lie, remove a block and talk about how to rebuild. End the week by celebrating how tall your "trust tower" can grow with truth.

PRAYER

God of truth, help us love what is honest. Give us courage to tell the truth and humility to make things right when we don't. In Jesus' name, Amen.

Week 11: Peace over Worry

"do not be anxious about anything" — Philippians 4:6 (ESV)

OPENING THOUGHT

Worry knots our stomachs. God invites us to bring everything to Him—every test, bill, friendship, and question—and to receive His peace.

FAMILY STORY

The Ramirez family budget meeting felt tense. Prices had climbed, and the car needed repairs. "What if we can't make it?" Mateo blurted. Mom put down her pen. "Let's name our worries and bring them to God."

They wrote worries on sticky notes and placed them in a bowl: "car repair," "soccer fees," "grandma's health." They prayed over each one, then made a simple plan—postpone a trip, sell a bike they'd outgrown, ask a neighbor about a car part discount.

During the week, the worries didn't vanish, but peace kept showing up. A friend offered a ride to practice. Grandma's checkup brought good news. The neighbor connected them with a mechanic who did the repair for less.

At week's end, they pulled the notes out and wrote a new word on each: "Provided," "Peace," "Still waiting." They realized peace wasn't the same as getting everything fixed fast. It was God's presence in the mess, turning knots into open hands.

DISCUSSION QUESTIONS

1. What do you worry about most? How does it feel to name it out loud?

2. What practical step could help with that worry—and how can we pray about it?

3. How have you experienced God's peace even before a problem was solved?

FAMILY ACTIVITY: WORRY TO PRAYER

Place a small basket in a central spot with index cards and pens. When worries pop up this week, write them down and place them in the basket. At meals or bedtime, take turns praying over a couple of cards. When you see movement, write a small note on the back and keep the card as a "peace story."

PRAYER

Father, we bring You our worries. Guard our hearts with Your peace as we trust You and take wise steps. In Jesus' name, Amen.

Week 12: Strength in Joy

"the joy of the LORD is your strength." —
Nehemiah 8:10 (ESV)

OPENING THOUGHT

Joy isn't the same as pretending life is perfect. It's a deep gladness rooted in God's goodness, and it gives us strength to face whatever comes.

FAMILY STORY

Coach Thompson's basketball team had lost three games in a row, and morale was wilted. Jada, the point guard, felt the weight of every missed shot. After practice, Coach gathered them at center court. "We'll keep working hard," she said, "but I want you to find joy in the game again. Play like you love it."

At the next game, Jada tied her shoes, closed her eyes, and breathed a short prayer: "God, help me play with Your joy." She ran the court with a lighter step, high-fiving teammates after good passes, not just good baskets. When Mia missed a layup, Jada grinned and shouted, "Next one's yours!" Mia laughed and nodded—and made the next one.

They didn't win that day, but something changed. The bench erupted for small victories. Parents noticed. "You guys looked alive out there," one dad said. Jada walked to the car with a tired body and a full heart. "Joy didn't fix the scoreboard," she told Mom, "but it gave me strength to keep playing."

DISCUSSION QUESTIONS

1. What brings you joy that isn't tied to winning or getting your way?

2. How can joy give strength during a hard week?

3. Where do you want to ask God for His joy right now?

FAMILY ACTIVITY: JOY JARS

Give each person a small jar. Throughout the week, write down "joy sparks" on slips of paper—moments that made you smile, laugh, or feel thankful. At week's end, pour them out and read them aloud. Talk about how joy showed up in expected and surprising places.

PRAYER

God, thank You for joy that strengthens us. Fill our hearts with Your joy and help us share it wherever we go. In Jesus' name, Amen.

Week 13: God Is Our Shepherd

"The LORD is my shepherd; I shall not want." —
Psalm 23:1 (ESV)

OPENING THOUGHT

Sheep don't navigate by themselves; they trust their shepherd. God leads, protects, and provides for us, even when the path winds through shadowy places.

FAMILY STORY

When the Whitakers visited a farm, they met Daisy, a woolly sheep with a curious nose. The farmer explained how his sheep recognized his voice. "If I call, they come. If a stranger calls, they stare." He whistled, and Daisy trotted over, bumping his leg for a scratch.

That night, nine-year-old Ben had a nightmare about getting lost at the county fair. He woke up breathless, heart pounding. Mom sat beside him. "Do you remember Daisy?" she asked. "She came when she heard her shepherd's voice." Ben nodded. They whispered Psalm 23:1 together.

The next day at the actual county fair, the crowds were big and noisy. Ben squeezed Dad's hand tighter. When he got jostled in the petting zoo and lost sight of his parents for a moment, panic buzzed. Then he heard Dad's whistle—three quick notes. Ben froze, listened, and followed the sound. He rounded a corner and saw Dad waving. Relief washed over him.

That night, Ben taped a note above his bed: "Listen for the Shepherd." He started learning God's voice by reading Scripture, praying, and paying attention to the steady peace that nudged him toward the right path.

DISCUSSION QUESTIONS

1. What helps you recognize God's voice in your life?

2. Where do you need to trust God to lead and provide right now?

3. How can our family "listen for the Shepherd" together this week?

FAMILY ACTIVITY: FOLLOW THE VOICE

Play a simple game: one person (the "shepherd") stands in another room and calls out short instructions ("two steps forward," "turn left"). The others, eyes closed, try to follow just the shepherd's voice while others softly call random directions. Talk about how it felt to focus on the right voice and how God's Word helps us do that daily.

PRAYER

Good Shepherd, thank You for leading and caring for us. Help us listen for Your voice and follow wherever You guide. In Jesus' name, Amen.

Week 14: Hope That Anchors

"We have this as a sure and steadfast anchor of the soul" — Hebrews 6:19 (ESV)

OPENING THOUGHT

Storms will come, but hope in God holds us steady. Not wishful thinking—real hope rooted in His promises and character.

FAMILY STORY

The Cho family loved boating on the lake. One afternoon, a sudden storm rolled in. Wind whipped the water into waves, and the sky turned charcoal. Dad quickly dropped the anchor. The boat still rocked, but it held.

Back home, they talked about another kind of storm. Grandma had just started chemo, and fear hovered. "What anchors us?" Mom asked. They listed promises: God is with us, He hears our prayers, He is faithful. They wrote them on paper anchors and taped them to the fridge.

Over the next months, there were good days and hard days. On the hard days, the family would point to the anchors and repeat them aloud. When Grandma lost her hair, she joked about finally saving on shampoo, and they laughed-crying together. When test results improved, they cheered. When they didn't, they clung to their anchors.

The lake storm passed, and so did some of the fear. The boat didn't sail backward to where it began; it moved forward through the storm—tethered by hope.

DISCUSSION QUESTIONS

1. What promise of God anchors you when life feels stormy?

2. Where do you need hope right now?

3. How can we remind each other of our "anchors" this week?

FAMILY ACTIVITY: ANCHOR WALL

Cut out paper anchors. On each, write a specific promise from Scripture or a truth about God (e.g., "God is with me," "God provides," "God is faithful"). Tape them in a visible place. When challenges arise this week, point to an anchor and pray that truth together.

PRAYER

God of hope, anchor our hearts in Your promises. Hold us steady in every storm and lead us forward in trust. In Jesus' name, Amen.

Week 15: Wise Choices

"If any of you lacks wisdom, let him ask God" —
James 1:5 (ESV)

OPENING THOUGHT

Wisdom isn't just knowing facts; it's knowing how to live God's way. When we ask, He gives generously—guiding our choices big and small.

FAMILY STORY

Chloe had to choose between two after-school clubs: robotics or dance. Both met on Tuesdays, both had friends she liked, and both would take time away from homework and family dinners. "I wish someone would just decide for me," she groaned.

Her mom suggested the "Three-Lights Test": God's Word, wise counsel, and inner peace. First, they looked at Scripture for principles—stewarding gifts, commitment, and balance. Then Chloe called Aunt Jen, who knew both her love for music and her knack for tinkering. "Which one helps you serve others right now?" Aunt Jen asked. Finally, Chloe prayed and paid attention to the peace in her heart.

The next morning, Chloe realized robotics would help her mentor younger students at the community center, and the schedule left space for rest. She felt a quiet yes. She chose robotics and wrote a note to the dance teacher about maybe joining in the spring.

A week later, Chloe helped a fourth-grader build a tiny solar car. Watching it zip forward, she smiled. Wisdom hadn't shouted; it had gently guided her steps.

DISCUSSION QUESTIONS

1. What big or small decision are you facing right now?

2. How can God's Word, wise people, and inner peace help you decide?

3. How can our family practice asking God for wisdom together?

FAMILY ACTIVITY: WISDOM BOARD

Create a simple decision board with three columns: God's Word, Wise Counsel, Peace. When a choice comes up this week, write it at the top and fill each column—find a verse, ask two trusted people for input, and note how your heart feels after prayer. Review together and make your next step with faith.

PRAYER

Generous God, we ask You for wisdom. Teach us to listen, think, and choose in ways that honor You and bless others. In Jesus' name, Amen.

Week 16: Friends That Last

"A friend loves at all times, and a brother is born for adversity." — Proverbs 17:17 (ESV)

OPENING THOUGHT

Good friends aren't just fun; they're faithful. God designed friendship to be a place where love shows up in ordinary days and especially when life gets tough.

FAMILY STORY

When the new semester started, Harper noticed that her best friend, Layla, stopped sitting with her at lunch. Layla seemed quieter, checking her phone and staring at the table. Harper guessed she'd done something wrong and started avoiding her, too. By Friday, their group chat was silent.

At youth group that weekend, their leader talked about "leaning in, not pulling away." Harper thought about the theme verse: friends love at all times—sunny times and stormy ones. On Monday, she took a deep breath and walked over to Layla before class. "I miss you," she said. "Did I do something?"

Layla's eyes filled with tears. "My mom lost her job," she whispered. "I've been embarrassed and stressed. I didn't want to talk to anyone." The problem wasn't Harper; it was a hidden storm. Harper's shoulders softened. "I'm so sorry. Can I sit with you today?"

That afternoon, Harper asked her parents if Layla could come over for dinner. They played board games and laughed until the worries loosened. Later, Harper texted, "I'm here for you.

All the times." Layla sent back a heart and a prayer hands emoji.

Their friendship didn't depend on perfect moods or perfect weeks; it grew deeper because love stayed. In adversity, they discovered what "at all times" means.

DISCUSSION QUESTIONS

1. What makes a friendship strong during hard times?

2. Have you ever pulled away when a friend needed you? What could you do differently next time?

3. Who might need you to "lean in" this week?

FAMILY ACTIVITY: FRIENDSHIP FIRST AID KIT

Create a small "friendship kit" together: note cards for encouragement, a few tea bags or hot cocoa packets, a fun sticker sheet, and a small list of uplifting verses. Each person chooses one friend to bless this week and delivers the kit with a kind note. Pray for each friend by name before you deliver.

PRAYER

Lord, thank You for faithful friends and for being our truest Friend. Teach us to love "at all times" and to show up when others face adversity. In Jesus' name, Amen.

Week 17: Honoring Parents, Honoring God

"Children, obey your parents in the Lord, for this
is right." — Ephesians 6:1 (ESV)

OPENING THOUGHT

Obedience isn't about control; it's about trust and safety. God places parents to guide us, and honoring them trains our hearts to honor God.

FAMILY STORY

Saturday chores had a way of turning into negotiations in the Bell household. This time, Micah argued that vacuuming was "not his talent" and should be reassigned to his sister, June, who "was practically a vacuum expert." Mom smiled. "Nice try."

After a few minutes of complaining, Micah finally vacuumed—fast, with zigzag lightning lines and a few missed corners. When he was done, he flopped on the couch. Dad sat beside him. "Can I tell you a story?" he asked. "When I was your age, Grandpa asked me to wash the car. I did it so fast the windows were streaky. Grandpa brought me back out and said, 'Obedience isn't rushing through; it's doing it with respect.' That stuck with me."

Micah frowned. "So I have to like vacuuming?" Dad shook his head. "You won't always like the task. Honoring means you care about the person asking—and you do your best."

Micah stood up, plugged the vacuum back in, and slowly finished the corners. It wasn't glorious, but afterward he felt a quiet pride. June noticed and said, "Thanks for doing it right. It helps all of us." Micah realized obedience didn't shrink him; it shaped him to love well.

DISCUSSION QUESTIONS

1. What helps you respond respectfully when you don't feel like obeying?

2. How does honoring parents prepare us to honor God's leadership?

3. Parents: how can you give instructions in ways that are clear, fair, and loving?

FAMILY ACTIVITY: THE HONOR CHALLENGE

Pick one common request (homework time, screen limits, chores). For one week, practice "first-time, full-heart" responses: listen, say "Okay," and do the task well. Parents commit to giving one encouraging sentence for each "honor moment." Keep a tally and celebrate with a simple family treat at week's end.

PRAYER

Father, thank You for the gift of family. Help children honor and obey with willing hearts, and help parents lead with wisdom and gentleness. In Jesus' name, Amen.

Week 18: Work as Worship

"Whatever you do, work heartily, as for the Lord and not for men," — Colossians 3:23 (ESV)

OPENING THOUGHT

Homework, dishwashing, coaching, and emails can all become worship when we offer our best to God. He is present in ordinary tasks, turning effort into love.

FAMILY STORY

Tia loved art projects but dragged her feet on math. One Tuesday, her teacher announced a surprise "clean desk check." Tia's desk looked like a paper volcano. At home, Mom introduced a new idea: "Work as worship." She drew a triangle: God at the top, Tia at one corner, her work at the other. "When you do your work for God, not just for a grade, it changes your heart."

The next afternoon, Tia set a timer for 20 minutes and organized one section of her desk. She whispered, "For You, God." It felt small, but she finished without grumbling. She tried the same with math homework, adding colorful tabs and asking Dad one focused question instead of five scattered ones. The work didn't become easy, but it felt purposeful.

On Friday, the teacher smiled. "Your desk looks great!" Tia's grade improved a bit, but the bigger win was her attitude. She even surprised herself by doing the dinner dishes while humming a worship song. She learned that worship wasn't only on Sunday; it was in every honest effort, done with love.

DISCUSSION QUESTIONS

1. What task do you dread? How might "work as worship" change it?

2. Parents and kids: what is one specific way to offer your work to God this week?

3. How can we encourage each other when tasks feel tedious?

FAMILY ACTIVITY: WORSHIP AT WORK PLAYLIST

Build a family playlist of worship and uplifting songs. Pick one daily task (homework, cleanup, meal prep) and play the playlist during that time. Begin with a one-sentence prayer: "God, we offer this work to You." End by sharing one thing you learned or noticed.

PRAYER

God, thank You for meaningful work. Teach us to work heartily for You, turning ordinary tasks into acts of love. In Jesus' name, Amen.

Week 19: Rest That Restores

"And he said to them, 'The Sabbath was made for man, not man for the Sabbath.'" — Mark 2:27 (ESV)

OPENING THOUGHT

God designed rest as a gift, not a burden. Sabbath isn't about rules; it's about breathing, delighting, and trusting God to run the world while we stop.

FAMILY STORY

The Chen family calendar looked like confetti—colorful boxes packed into every day. One Friday night, Dad called for a family meeting. "We're tired. What if we try a Sabbath from Saturday evening to Sunday evening? No chores, no shopping, no heavy talk. Just worship, rest, and delight."

They lit a candle to begin. Mom prayed, "We rest because You are God and we are not." On Saturday night, they played cards, read books, and took a slow walk around the block. Sunday morning, they went to church, then napped and drew on the porch. When an email dinged, Dad silenced his phone. "It can wait," he said, smiling.

It wasn't perfect. The dog knocked over the candle, and the dishwasher broke. But the day felt different—unhurried and full of breath. By Sunday evening, they blew out the candle and shared highlights. "I felt like my brain took a deep sigh,"

Emma said. They returned to Monday lighter, discovering that rest wasn't wasted time; it was a way to trust God more.

DISCUSSION QUESTIONS

1. What makes it hard to rest? What helps you feel restored?

2. What would a life-giving Sabbath look like for our family in this season?

3. How does resting increase our trust in God?

FAMILY ACTIVITY: SABBATH BOX

Decorate a box labeled "Sabbath." Before your rest time, place inside items that represent work and hurry (devices, to-do lists). Add rest items nearby: a favorite book, art supplies, a nature guide. Begin with a short prayer and end by sharing one delight from your Sabbath.

Safety note: If young children are present, use an LED/battery candle instead of an open flame, and keep any candles out of reach and supervised at all times.

PRAYER

Creator God, thank You for the gift of rest. Teach us to stop, delight, and trust You. Restore our bodies and hearts. In Jesus' name, Amen.

Week 20: Cheerful Giving

"Each one must give as he has decided in his heart, not reluctantly or under compulsion, for God loves a cheerful giver." — 2 Corinthians 9:7 (ESV)

OPENING THOUGHT

Giving isn't about the size of the gift but the spirit behind it. God's generosity toward us spills over into joyful, willing giving.

FAMILY STORY

When their church launched a backpack drive for local students, the Brooks family decided each person would fill one backpack. Zoe picked bright teal. She calculated how many pencils, notebooks, and snacks she could buy with her allowance. Halfway through the store, she hesitated. "If I spend this much, I can't buy the nail polish I wanted."

Dad knelt beside her. "You get to decide. What kind of giver do you want to be?" Zoe stared at the teal backpack, picturing a kid opening it on the first day of school. "Cheerful," she said quietly. She grabbed a pack of colorful pens and a note card set. At home, she wrote a note: "You've got this. I'm cheering for you."

On delivery day, the organizer shared stories of kids who would receive the bags. Zoe felt a warm joy that nail polish couldn't match. She learned that cheerful giving isn't reluctant or forced; it's a choice that fills both the giver and the receiver.

DISCUSSION QUESTIONS

1. When have you felt cheerful about giving? What made it joyful?

2. What keeps us from giving generously—fear, comparison, or something else?

3. What is one way our family can give this week—time, money, or kindness?

FAMILY ACTIVITY: THE GIVE, SAVE, SPEND JARS

Set up three jars for each family member: Give, Save, Spend. Decide together what portion goes into each when money comes in (allowance, gifts). Choose a cause or person to bless from the Give jar this month. Share updates on how your giving is making an impact.

PRAYER

Generous God, thank You for giving us everything in Jesus. Make our hearts cheerful and open-handed so others can experience Your love through us. In Jesus' name, Amen.

Week 21: Words That Heal

"A soft answer turns away wrath, but a harsh word stirs up anger." — Proverbs 15:1 (ESV)

OPENING THOUGHT

Words can be like bandages or like thorns. With God's help, our mouths can bring calm, not chaos—especially when tempers flare.

FAMILY STORY

During an intense board game, brothers Carter and Miles argued about a rule. Voices rose; the dog hid under the table. Mom stepped in. "Pause. Try 'soft answers.'" Carter rolled his eyes. "He's wrong!" Miles crossed his arms. "I'm not."

They took a breath. Carter tried again. "I feel frustrated because the last time we played, we used this rule." Miles softened. "I thought we changed it." They looked up the rule together and realized they'd both remembered parts. The tension melted.

Later that week, Carter used the same approach when a classmate teased him. Instead of snapping back, he said calmly, "That hurt. Please stop." The boy shrugged and backed off.

Carter was surprised. Soft didn't mean weak; it meant wise and strong.

By Saturday, "soft answer" became a family phrase. It didn't fix every problem, but it slowed the fire and made space for peace.

DISCUSSION QUESTIONS

1. When do harsh words come easily for you? What triggers them?

2. What are some "soft answers" you can prepare ahead of time?

3. How can we remind each other to choose words that heal?

FAMILY ACTIVITY: PHRASE BANK

Create a list of gentle, truthful phrases for tense moments: "I feel...," "Can we pause?," "Help me understand," "Let's find a solution together," "I need a minute." Hang the list on the fridge. Practice with simple role-plays. Celebrate real-life wins by adding a sticker next to the phrase used.

PRAYER

Lord, tame our tongues. Teach us to answer gently, speak truthfully, and heal with our words. In Jesus' name, Amen.

Week 22: Children of God

"See what kind of love the Father has given to us, that we should be called children of God; and so we are." — 1 John 3:1 (ESV)

OPENING THOUGHT

Our identity isn't built on grades, goals, or how many friends we have. In Christ, we are God's beloved children—deeply known and securely loved.

FAMILY STORY

At the beginning of middle school, Lily tried out three different "looks" in one week: sporty Lily, artsy Lily, and Lily-who-said-yes-to-everything. She was exhausted by Friday, unsure who she was. That night, her grandma visited and brought an old photo album.

They flipped to a page where toddler Lily wore a spaghetti-sauce smile. "You were always mine," Grandma whispered. "Not because you were clean or tidy, but because you were loved." She pointed to the verse on the fridge: children of God.

On Sunday, Lily heard a sermon about being adopted into God's family through Jesus. She realized she didn't have to earn a place at God's table. She already had one. On Monday, she wore her favorite jeans and a paint-splattered hoodie, said no to one club, and yes to art class. She texted a friend, "I'm learning to be me—the me God loves."

Her week didn't become perfect, but it became lighter. Being God's child gave her courage to show up as herself.

DISCUSSION QUESTIONS

1. What labels do you tend to wear (smart, athletic, shy)? Which ones feel heavy?

2. How does being "children of God" change how we see ourselves and others?

3. What's one brave choice you can make from a place of secure identity this week?

FAMILY ACTIVITY: NAME CARDS

Make simple "family name cards." On one side, write your first name. On the other, write "Child of God" with three truths underneath (Loved, Forgiven, Called). Place them at the dinner table each night this week. Start meals by reading the truths aloud together.

PRAYER

Father, thank You for calling us Your children. Root our identity in Your love and free us to live honestly and boldly. In Jesus' name, Amen.

Week 23: Don't Give Up

"And let us not grow weary of doing good, for in due season we will reap, if we do not give up." — Galatians 6:9 (ESV)

OPENING THOUGHT

Good seeds take time to grow. When doing the right thing feels unnoticed or tiring, God reminds us: keep going—harvest is coming.

FAMILY STORY

Jamal volunteered to tutor a younger student, Evan, who struggled with reading. The first few sessions felt like pedaling a bike uphill. Evan mixed up letters, lost focus, and sometimes declared, "I'm done." Jamal went home discouraged.

His aunt, a gardener, listened over tea. "When I plant carrots, I don't see anything for weeks," she said. "But underground, roots are growing." She encouraged Jamal to celebrate tiny wins.

At the next session, they cheered for every correct sound and took short breaks to do silly stretches. When Evan read a full page without stopping, he grinned. "I did it!" Weeks later, Evan read an entire short book. He hugged Jamal's arm. "Thanks for not giving up."

Jamal realized that perseverance isn't loud. It's steady love that keeps showing up, believing that God brings growth in His timing.

DISCUSSION QUESTIONS

1. Where do you feel tempted to give up right now?

2. What "tiny wins" can we celebrate to keep going?

3. Who needs our steady encouragement this week?

FAMILY ACTIVITY: GROWTH CHART

Choose one area to persevere in (prayer, reading, exercise, kindness). Create a simple chart with daily boxes for the week. Each day you practice, color a box and write one small win. At week's end, thank God for growth and talk about the "roots" He's growing that you can't yet see.

PRAYER

Lord, strengthen our hands to keep doing good. Help us trust Your timing and rejoice in every bit of growth. In Jesus' name, Amen.

Week 24: Do Justice, Love Kindness

"He has told you, O man, what is good; and what does the LORD require of you but to do justice, and to love kindness, and to walk humbly with your God?" — Micah 6:8 (ESV)

OPENING THOUGHT

God's heart beats for what's right, compassionate, and humble. As His people, we practice fairness, kindness, and a posture of walking with Him.

FAMILY STORY

At recess, Naomi noticed that the same kids always got picked first for soccer, while others waited and rarely played. She felt a nudge to speak up, but fear whispered, "Don't rock the boat." That night, she told her parents. They talked about doing justice (what's right), loving kindness (how we do it), and walking humbly (our attitude).

The next day, Naomi asked the teacher if she could help organize teams. They tried a new system: rotating captains and a rule that everyone plays before any one person gets a second turn. At first, the "top players" groaned. But soon, the game felt more fun. New players discovered hidden talent, and the sidelines cheered louder.

Later, one of the overlooked kids told Naomi, "Thanks for noticing." Naomi realized justice wasn't about being loud; it was about using her voice to help others be seen—and doing it with kindness and humility.

DISCUSSION QUESTIONS

1. Where do you see unfairness at school, work, or in our community?

2. What's one small step we can take to "do justice" this week?

3. How do kindness and humility shape the way we pursue what's right?

FAMILY ACTIVITY: KIND JUSTICE PROJECT

Choose one local need (food insecurity, inclusion at school, litter at a park). Plan a simple action: assemble snack packs, start an inclusive game, or host a neighborhood clean-up. Begin with prayer for the people affected. Afterward, reflect: What did we learn? How can we continue?

PRAYER

Righteous God, give us eyes to see injustice and hearts to act with kindness and humility. Lead us to love people the way You do. In Jesus' name, Amen.

Week 25: Open Doors of Hospitality

"Do not neglect to show hospitality to strangers, for thereby some have entertained angels unawares." — Hebrews 13:2 (ESV)

OPENING THOUGHT

Hospitality isn't about fancy plates—it's about open doors and warm hearts. God welcomes us; we get to pass that welcome along.

FAMILY STORY

When a new family moved into the cul-de-sac, the Parkers noticed cardboard boxes and tired faces. Mom said, "Let's bring dinner." The kids voted for chili and cornbread. They wrote a note: "Welcome to the neighborhood! —The Parkers."

They carried the food over, and a boy about their age opened the door. "I'm Theo," he said shyly. Inside, they saw a fort made of boxes and a dog wagging so hard his tail thumped like a drum. They chatted for a few minutes, then headed home.

A week later, Theo knocked on their door with homemade cookies and a handwritten map of the neighborhood: best sledding hill, friendliest cat, shortcut to the park. The families started Friday game nights, swapping snacks and stories. Hospitality didn't require a perfect house; it required willing hearts. Their open door opened friendships that felt like a gift from God.

DISCUSSION QUESTIONS

1. What keeps us from inviting people in—fear, mess, or busyness?

2. What simple welcome could we offer someone this week?

3. How does God's welcome to us inspire our hospitality?

FAMILY ACTIVITY: THREE-MINUTE TIDY, OPEN-DOOR INVITE

Choose one evening to invite a neighbor or friend. Do a three-minute tidy together—set a timer and everyone picks up quickly. Prepare simple snacks and a conversation jar with fun questions. Pray before they arrive: "God, let our home be a place of peace and welcome."

PRAYER

Welcoming God, thank You for inviting us into Your family. Help us open our doors and hearts so others can experience Your love. In Jesus' name, Amen.

Week 26: Care for God's Creation

"The LORD God took the man and put him in the garden of Eden to work it and keep it." — Genesis 2:15 (ESV)

OPENING THOUGHT

God made a beautiful world and asked us to care for it. Stewardship means tending creation with gratitude, wisdom, and hope.

FAMILY STORY

After a storm, the Rivera family walked their favorite trail and found it littered with plastic and fallen branches. Eight-year-old Mateo frowned. "This used to be our butterfly spot." Mom nodded. "Maybe we can help restore it."

They returned the next day with gloves, bags, and a rake. As they worked, a jogger slowed and asked, "Doing a cleanup?" Soon, three neighbors joined in. They found a caterpillar inching along a leaf and carefully moved it to a safe spot. Someone brought lemonade. By afternoon, the trail looked like itself again—soft and green.

The next week, butterflies returned to the milkweed. Mateo watched one land, wings like stained glass. "We kept our garden," he whispered, thinking of the verse. Caring for creation wasn't a burden; it was a way to love the God who made it.

DISCUSSION QUESTIONS

1. What part of creation helps you worship God?

2. What small habits can we practice to "work and keep" our corner of the world?

3. How can we invite others to join us in caring for creation?

FAMILY ACTIVITY: CREATION STEWARDSHIP DAY

Pick a project: park cleanup, planting native flowers, starting a small compost, or reducing single-use plastics for a week. Take before-and-after photos. Pray on site, thanking God for His world and asking for wisdom to care for it well.

PRAYER

Maker of heaven and earth, thank You for Your beautiful creation. Teach us to work and keep it with care and joy. In Jesus' name, Amen.

Week 27: Walking in Humility

"Do nothing from selfish ambition or conceit, but in humility count others more significant than yourselves." — Philippians 2:3 (ESV)

OPENING THOUGHT

Humility isn't thinking less of yourself; it's thinking of yourself less. Jesus shows us how to serve, listen, and lift others up.

FAMILY STORY

In group projects, Ava liked to lead. She had good ideas and wanted things done right. This time, her team was designing a science fair display. Ava assigned tasks quickly and corrected every font choice. Soon, her teammates stopped offering ideas. At lunch, she overheard someone say, "Why bother? She'll redo it anyway."

That night, Ava's dad told her about a boss who modeled humility. "He asked questions, gave credit, and admitted mistakes," Dad said. "People did their best work around him." Ava decided to try a different approach.

The next day, she asked her team, "What do you think?" She listened, even when ideas differed from hers. When someone made a great sketch, she highlighted it. When she realized she'd missed a measurement, she owned it. The project got better—and so did the team.

At the fair, they didn't win first place, but they won "Team Spirit." Ava learned that humility creates space for everyone to shine.

DISCUSSION QUESTIONS

1. Where do you find it hard to put others first?

2. What does humility look like at home, school, and work?

3. How did Jesus model humility—and how can we follow Him?

FAMILY ACTIVITY: THE "YOU FIRST" DAY

Choose a day where each person looks for one way to go second: let someone else choose the seat, snack, or show; ask a question before sharing your opinion. At dinner, share moments when humility opened a door for kindness or creativity.

PRAYER

Jesus, humble King, teach us to value others and to serve with joy. Free us from pride and help us walk in Your way. In Your name, Amen.

Week 28: When Disappointment Comes

"The LORD is near to the brokenhearted and saves the crushed in spirit." — Psalm 34:18 (ESV)

OPENING THOUGHT

God doesn't promise we'll always get what we want, but He promises His nearness. He meets us in disappointment with comfort and hope.

FAMILY STORY

Nora trained for months to make the swim team. Tryouts were tough, but she felt strong—until the results came out. Her name wasn't on the list. She held it together until she got home, then cried on the kitchen floor. Mom sat beside her in silence, handing her tissues.

After a while, Mom read the verse softly. "The Lord is near." They talked about what hurt the most: the lost dream, the fear of what friends would say, the feeling of not being enough. Dad suggested taking a week to rest, then reevaluate. "Your worth isn't in a roster," he said gently.

Nora decided to keep swimming with a community club and to help teach younger kids on Saturday mornings. She found unexpected joy in encouraging others. The disappointment didn't vanish, but God's nearness became real in new ways—

through family, Scripture, and a pool full of splashes and laughter.

DISCUSSION QUESTIONS

1. What disappointment are you carrying now? What do you need from God and from us?

2. How have you sensed God's nearness in hard moments before?

3. What new paths might God open when a door closes?

FAMILY ACTIVITY: LAMENT AND LIFT

Set out paper and pens. Each person writes a short "lament" prayer: name the disappointment honestly, then ask for God's help. Fold the paper and place it under a small cross or a candle. Later in the week, write a "lift" note—where you've seen God's nearness—and place it beside the first.

Safety note: If young children are present, use an LED/battery candle instead of an open flame, and keep any candles out of reach and supervised at all times.

PRAYER

Comforting God, draw near to our broken hearts. Hold us, heal us, and lead us to hope that doesn't disappoint. In Jesus' name, Amen.

Week 29: Sharing Our Hope

"but in your hearts honor Christ the Lord as holy, always being prepared to make a defense to anyone who asks you for a reason for the hope that is in you; yet do it with gentleness and respect," — 1 Peter 3:15 (ESV)

OPENING THOUGHT

We don't push or pressure; we share the hope we've found in Jesus with humility. Our lives and words can point others to Him.

FAMILY STORY

When his class discussed "What gives your life meaning?" Elijah hesitated. He loved Jesus, but he didn't want to sound preachy. He remembered the verse about gentleness and respect. When it was his turn, he said, "My hope comes from Jesus. He forgives me and helps me love others. If you're curious, I'm happy to talk more."

After class, a classmate named Jonah whispered, "My grandpa's sick. Could you pray?" Elijah nodded. They sat on the steps and prayed quietly. Later, Jonah texted, "Thanks. That meant a lot." A week after that, another student asked Elijah why he seemed peaceful during a tough test week. Elijah shared how prayer and Scripture helped him.

Elijah learned that sharing faith isn't about winning arguments; it's about honoring Christ in your heart and being ready when people ask. The tone matters as much as the truth: gentleness and respect open doors.

DISCUSSION QUESTIONS

1. Who in your life might be curious about your hope?

2. What's your short "hope story" you could share in 30 seconds?

3. How can we keep our tone gentle and respectful when we talk about Jesus?

FAMILY ACTIVITY: HOPE IN THREE LINES

Each person writes three simple lines: Before Jesus (or before hope felt real), Meeting Jesus, Life with Jesus now. Practice saying it kindly and clearly. Pray for one person who might need hope and ask God for a natural moment to share.

PRAYER

Jesus, thank You for being our hope. Make us ready to share Your love with gentleness and respect, and draw hearts to Yourself. In Your name, Amen.

Week 30: Bound Together in Love

"And above all these put on love, which binds everything together in perfect harmony." — Colossians 3:14 (ESV)

OPENING THOUGHT

Families and churches are a mix of personalities, preferences, and quirks. Love is the bond that holds us together—stronger than our differences.

FAMILY STORY

The Daniels family had a "Great Playlist Debate" every road trip. Dad liked classic rock, Mom preferred podcasts, Emma loved pop, and Liam wanted audiobooks about dragons. The car became a battlefield on wheels. After one especially noisy debate, Mom suggested a new plan: "Let's put on love."

They made a rotation and, more importantly, a new rule: whoever's turn it was would be honored—no mocking, no groaning, one genuine question about why they chose it. At first, the smiles were stiff. But as they listened, they learned. Mom discovered she liked one of Emma's artists. Dad and Liam laughed at the same dragon narrator. Emma asked a thoughtful question about Mom's podcast, and Mom beamed.

Love didn't mean pretending to like everything; it meant choosing harmony over winning. By the time they reached Grandma's house, the car felt more like a choir than a contest.

DISCUSSION QUESTIONS

1. Where do our differences cause friction at home?

2. What would it look like to "put on love" in those moments?

3. How can we honor each person's voice while pursuing harmony?

FAMILY ACTIVITY: HARMONY NIGHT

Plan an evening where each person contributes one element: a song, a snack, a game, or a topic. Commit to honoring each choice with curiosity and kindness. End by sharing one compliment for each person about what they brought to the table.

PRAYER

God of love, bind our family together in harmony. Teach us to honor one another and to choose love over winning. In Jesus' name, Amen.

Week 31: Faith Over Fear

"fear not, for I am with you; be not dismayed, for I
am your God; I will strengthen you, I will help you,"
— Isaiah 41:10 (ESV)

OPENING THOUGHT

Fear shouts, but God speaks steady. He doesn't promise a life
without scary things—He promises His presence in the middle
of them. Faith is choosing to hold His hand when our knees
shake.

FAMILY STORY

The Carters were moving across town. New school, new
church, new everything. Nine-year-old Quinn packed her
favorite books into a box labeled "Comfort." She tried to be
brave, but at night her stomach fluttered.

On the first day at the new school, Quinn's class walked into
music and the teacher announced a group rhythm activity.
"Find a partner!" came the call. Quinn froze. Everyone seemed
to pair up in a blink. She stood there, trying to look busy. A
boy named Jace noticed and waved. "Want to join us?" She
nodded, relief tumbling out as a breath.

At lunch, the cafeteria sounded like a hundred trains. Quinn
sat with Jace's group and learned they loved the same mystery
series. On the bus ride home, she whispered Isaiah 41:10 that
Mom had written on a sticky note in her lunchbox: "Fear not...
I am with you." That night she stuck the note to the head-
board.

The next morning, Quinn packed courage into her backpack—
right next to her math homework. When her heart wobbled

again during recess, she squeezed the sticky note and prayed, "God, hold me." She didn't become fearless; she became "held." And held was enough to take the next step, and the next.

DISCUSSION QUESTIONS

1. What situation makes you feel afraid right now? What would it look like to be "held" by God in it?

2. When have you seen God give strength in a scary moment?

3. How can we remind each other of God's presence when fear shouts?

FAMILY ACTIVITY: "FEAR NOT" FORT

Build a simple blanket fort. Inside, share one fear each. Then tape a few short promises (Isaiah 41:10, Psalm 56:3, John 14:27) to the "walls." Take turns reading them aloud like a little litany. End by switching off the room lights and turning on a small lamp to picture God's presence. Keep one verse card by each person's bed this week.

PRAYER

Father, when fear rises, remind us You are near. Strengthen our hearts and steady our steps as we trust You. In Jesus' name, Amen.

Week 32: Self-Control in the Moment

"A man without self-control is like a city broken into and left without walls." — Proverbs 25:28 (ESV)

OPENING THOUGHT

Self-control isn't just saying no; it's saying yes to a better way. With God's help, our emotions and appetites don't have to run the show.

FAMILY STORY

During the Mitchells' game night, competitive sparks sometimes flew. This time, twelve-year-old Rowan lost a close round of Dutch Blitz and slammed his cards. "It's not fair!" he snapped at his sister, Skye. The room went quiet.

Dad pulled out a napkin and drew a little city with walls. "Think of self-control like city walls," he said. "They don't keep out joy. They keep out things that would wreck the town."

Rowan groaned. "So I'm a wall-less city?" Mom smiled gently. "Right now, your anger knocked a gate off. But gates can be rebuilt." They brainstormed "gate repairs" for heated moments: breathe prayer, count to ten, take a pause walk, name the feeling.

The next day, Rowan practiced. When a classmate snagged the last chocolate milk, he felt the "storm." He whispered, "Jesus, help me," counted to ten, and grabbed plain milk. Not glamorous, but he didn't lash out. That evening at game night, he lost a round and surprised himself by saying, "Good game." Skye blinked, then grinned. The walls were going back up—brick by brick.

DISCUSSION QUESTIONS

1. When do you feel your "city walls" wobble—screens, snacks, sarcasm, anger?

2. What practical "gate repairs" could help you in the moment?

3. How can we cheer each other on as God strengthens our self-control?

FAMILY ACTIVITY: PAUSE TOKENS

Cut out five small "pause tokens" for each person. When emotions spike, anyone can hand a token to themselves or another, signaling a two-minute reset: breathe, pray, get water, step outside. At day's end, share one moment a token helped and one small win. Replace used tokens weekly.

PRAYER

Holy Spirit, grow self-control in us. Give us strength to pause, choose wisely, and love well—especially when it's hard. In Jesus' name, Amen.

Week 33: Quick to Listen

"let every person be quick to hear, slow to speak,
slow to anger;" — James 1:19 (ESV)

OPENING THOUGHT

Listening is love with ears. When we slow our words and anger, we make room for understanding and peace.

FAMILY STORY

During a neighborhood planning meeting, the Lopez family discussed turning a vacant lot into a community garden. Opinions sprouted like weeds. Miguel, age 10, tugged Mom's sleeve. "Everyone's talking, no one's listening."

Their neighbor Mr. Dean stood up to speak. He was often gruff, and Miguel braced for a rant. But Mr. Dean surprised everyone. "I've lived here forty years," he said slowly. "My late wife loved roses. I'd like to plant one bush for her." The room softened.

Miguel raised his hand and said, "Could we have a rose corner for people we miss?" Heads nodded. The meeting shifted from debate to design. Later, as they walked home, Mom said, "Listening changed the room." Miguel thought about school arguments and family squabbles. Maybe quick-to-hear was a superpower.

The garden opened in spring with a small sign: "Ruth's Roses." On planting day, Mr. Dean showed Miguel how to dig a proper hole and water deeply. Miguel learned that listening doesn't silence us; it gives our words richer soil.

DISCUSSION QUESTIONS

1. What gets in the way of listening—interrupting, assuming, getting defensive?

2. What's one situation this week where you can practice being "quick to hear"?

3. How does listening first change the outcome of conflicts?

FAMILY ACTIVITY: THE LISTENING TIMER

Use a two-minute sand timer. When someone shares, they get the timer and everyone else only listens—no fixing, no advice—until the sand runs out. Then others can ask clarifying questions. Try it during dinner stories or when resolving a conflict. Notice how it feels to be heard.

PRAYER

Lord, slow our mouths and steady our hearts. Make us quick to listen so we can love well and live wisely. In Jesus' name, Amen.

Week 34: United in Christ

"eager to maintain the unity of the Spirit in the bond of peace." — Ephesians 4:3 (ESV)

OPENING THOUGHT

Unity isn't sameness; it's harmony around Jesus. We fight for peace not by winning arguments, but by loving one another well.

FAMILY STORY

The Gaines family loved their church, but a change in worship style stirred mixed feelings. Grandma missed hymns, Dad liked the new songs, and the teens just wanted volume turned down two notches. After a bumpy Sunday, they ate pancakes and talked.

Grandma said, "When I was a girl, we argued about pew cushions." Everyone laughed. She added, "But you know what? The gospel stayed the same." They decided to write a "unity plan": pray for leaders, prefer one another in small ways (let someone else choose where to sit), and encourage at least one person every Sunday.

The next week, Grandma asked the worship leader about including a hymn occasionally. He listened kindly and agreed to weave one in. Dad sang the new song wholeheartedly. The teens served in kids' ministry with earplugs—and smiles. Love didn't erase differences, but it made space for them.

By month's end, the Gaines family had a new tradition: on the drive home, each person shared one way they saw unity at work—someone praying together across generations, a shared laugh over spilled coffee, a heartfelt story in small group. Unity became more than a word; it became their way.

DISCUSSION QUESTIONS

1. Where do differences threaten unity in our family or church?

2. What does it look like to be "eager" to maintain peace this week?

3. How can we put the gospel at the center when preferences differ?

FAMILY ACTIVITY: PEACE PUZZLES

Buy a simple puzzle. On the back of pieces, write actions that build unity (pray, encourage, listen, forgive, serve, compromise). Each time someone practices one, add a piece to complete the picture. When finished, display it briefly and thank God for knitting hearts together.

PRAYER

Jesus, our Peace, bind us together by Your Spirit. Help us choose love over preference and unity over winning. In Your name, Amen.

Week 35: Don't Lose Heart in Prayer

"And he told them a parable to the effect that they ought always to pray and not lose heart." — Luke 18:1 (ESV)

OPENING THOUGHT

Some answers come quickly; others take a long time. God invites us to keep praying—trusting His timing, wisdom, and love.

FAMILY STORY

When Uncle Ray deployed overseas, the Nguyen family began praying nightly for his safety. Weeks turned into months. Seven-year-old Ethan asked, "Does God get tired of hearing the same prayer?" Mom smiled. "Never."

They made a prayer map, placing a sticker where Uncle Ray served. Each night, they lit a candle and prayed for protection, courage, and peace for families on both sides of the conflict. Some nights their prayers felt strong; other nights they felt like whispers.

One evening, news of unrest near Uncle Ray's base rattled them. Ethan drew a shield on an index card and taped it near the map. "God, be his shield," he prayed. A week later, Uncle Ray called. "We had a close call, but we're okay," he said. The family exhaled, grateful and teary.

Months later, when Uncle Ray came home, they kept the map. "There are more people to pray for," Ethan said. They learned that persevering prayer wasn't magic—it was relationship.

They brought their hearts to God, again and again, and He held them.

DISCUSSION QUESTIONS

1. What have you been praying for a long time? How can we keep from losing heart?

2. How has God met you in prayer even before an answer came?

3. Who can we add to our prayer map this week?

FAMILY ACTIVITY: PRAYER MAP AND BEADS

Hang a simple world map. Write prayer requests on small sticky flags. Create a short prayer "bead" string (five beads for praise, confession, thanks, ask, others). Move through the beads together a few times a week, pointing to places on the map as you pray. Note dates when prayers are answered or when perspective changes.

PRAYER

Faithful God, teach us to pray and not lose heart. Strengthen our hope, align our desires with Yours, and keep us close to You. In Jesus' name, Amen.

Week 36: New Mercies Every Morning

"The steadfast love of the LORD never ceases; his mercies never come to an end; they are new every morning; great is your faithfulness." — Lamentations 3:22-23 (ESV)

OPENING THOUGHT

God's mercy isn't a tiny tube of toothpaste we ration. It's a fresh river every morning. Yesterday's failures don't get the final say.

FAMILY STORY

After a tough week of missed alarms and messy attitudes, the Bennetts declared Friday "do-over day." Mom poured cereal into bowls and said, "Let's start with mercy." Dad read Lamentations 3:22-23. Eleven-year-old Jonah sighed. "I really messed up in math yesterday."

Mom nodded. "And today has new mercies." Jonah decided to talk to his teacher. "I tried to rush the assignment and cheated by looking at an answer key online," he admitted. The teacher thanked him for his honesty and gave him a chance to redo the work with a small consequence. It wasn't easy, but it felt clean.

At home, the family made "Mercy Mornings" cards: short reminders like "Forgiven," "Fresh Start," "Try Again." They set them by toothbrushes and on the fridge. Over the next week, they reached for those cards after sibling squabbles, a spilled smoothie, and a forgotten practice. Mercy didn't remove consequences; it changed the tone—from shame to hope, from hiding to honesty.

By Sunday, Jonah said, "Mercy doesn't mean I get away with stuff. It means I don't have to stay stuck." The family nodded, grateful for a God whose faithfulness outlasts their failures.

DISCUSSION QUESTIONS

1. Where do you most need a fresh start right now?

2. How can we be "mercy givers" to each other at home?

3. What's the difference between cheap excuses and true mercy?

FAMILY ACTIVITY: MERCY MORNINGS BOX

Decorate a small box and fill it with "Mercy Mornings" cards with Scriptures and phrases. Each morning, draw one and read it aloud together. Commit to one "mercy practice" that day: apologize quickly, offer a redo, speak hope over someone's struggle. Share at dinner how mercy showed up.

PRAYER

God of mercy, thank You for new mercies every morning. Help us receive Your grace and pass it along freely. Great is Your faithfulness. In Jesus' name, Amen.

Week 37: Guard Your Thoughts

"Whatever is true, whatever is honorable, whatever is just, whatever is pure, whatever is lovely... think about these things." — Philippians 4:8 (ESV)

OPENING THOUGHT

Our minds are gardens. What we plant grows. With God's help, we can pull weeds of worry and dishonesty and cultivate thoughts that bring peace.

FAMILY STORY

On the bus, Taryn scrolled through posts that left her feeling less-than. By the time she got home, her thoughts were tangled: "I'm behind. I'm boring. I'm not enough." At dinner, Dad suggested a "thought swap." "What's one thought you want to trade for truth?" he asked.

Taryn shrugged, then said, "I'm not enough." Mom nodded. "Let's find what's true." They looked up Philippians 4:8 and talked about what God says: loved, chosen, created on purpose. Taryn wrote "I am God's workmanship" on a sticky note and put it on her mirror.

The next day, when the old thought crept in, she whispered, "Swap it." She turned off her feed for a while and took the dog for a walk. She noticed the sky painting itself with evening colors. "Whatever is lovely," she said out loud, smiling. She still liked her friends' updates, but she didn't let them define her.

By week's end, the family had a whole list of swaps—worry to prayer, comparison to gratitude, cynicism to curiosity. Their minds didn't become perfect, but their gardens looked less weedy and more alive.

DISCUSSION QUESTIONS

1. What "weed thoughts" pop up most for you? What truth can replace them?

2. How does what we watch and scroll affect our thinking?

3. What can our family do to plant more "true and lovely" thoughts this week?

FAMILY ACTIVITY: THOUGHT GARDEN

Draw a simple garden on poster board with a "Weeds" section and a "Seeds" section. Write weed thoughts on sticky notes and place them on the weeds. Then find Scriptures or truths to replace them and move new notes to the seeds. Water your "seeds" daily by speaking them aloud.

PRAYER

Lord, renew our minds. Help us think on what is true and lovely, and uproot lies and worries. In Jesus' name, Amen.

Week 38: Integrity Online

"Turn my eyes from looking at worthless things; and give me life in your ways." — Psalm 119:37 (ESV)

OPENING THOUGHT

Screens can bless or drain. Integrity means we choose what honors God—even when no one's watching—and we invite wise boundaries.

FAMILY STORY

After homework, Kayden disappeared into his room with a tablet. "Just a few videos," he said. Two hours later, his eyes felt foggy and his heart felt heavy. The content wasn't awful—but it wasn't good, either. It left him restless.

At dinner, Dad shared Psalm 119:37. "Let's make a family screen rule—made by us, not just handed down," he said. They created a simple plan: shared charging station at night, "why watch?" questions before clicking (Does it build up? Is it true? Will I feel more alive after?), and a weekly "digital sabbath" hour.

Kayden tried the "why watch?" practice the next day. When a recommended video looked sketchy, he whispered, "Turn my eyes," and closed the app. He picked up his guitar instead and learned a new chord progression. That night he felt clearer, less foggy.

By Friday, the whole family noticed a difference: better sleep, more conversation, and fewer edge-of-anger moments. Integrity online didn't make them anti-tech; it made them pro-life—the kind that grows when eyes are set on worthy things.

DISCUSSION QUESTIONS

1. What content drains you? What content brings life?

2. Which boundaries would help us honor God with our screens?

3. How can we encourage each other without shaming when we slip?

FAMILY ACTIVITY: SCREEN COVENANT

Write a simple, grace-filled family covenant: goals (honor God, protect hearts), boundaries (charging spot, time limits, "why watch?" questions), and repair steps (confess quickly, reset, try again). Everyone signs and posts it in a visible place. Review monthly and adjust together.

PRAYER

God, turn our eyes from worthless things. Give us wisdom and integrity online so our hearts stay rooted in Your ways. In Jesus' name, Amen.

Week 39: Number Our Days

"So teach us to number our days that we may get a heart of wisdom." — Psalm 90:12 (ESV)

OPENING THOUGHT

Time is a gift, not a guarantee. Wisdom learns to say yes to what matters and no to what drains, so we can live fully with God and one another.

FAMILY STORY

The Jeffersons realized they were saying "hurry up" more than "how was your day?" Soccer, piano, extra meetings—good things were crowding out best things. Mom brought out a paper plate and a marker. "Let's make a time pie," she said.

They sketched a normal week—sleep, school, work, activities, screens, chores, family, church, rest. The "screens" slice was bigger than expected. Dad said, "We can't add hours, but we can adjust the slices." They chose two shifts: a 20-minute nightly "family window" with no devices and a weekly "margin hour" for anything restful.

At first it felt strange to stop the scroll and play Uno or walk the dog together. But after a few days, the house sounded different—more laughter, less rushing. When an extra opportunity popped up, they asked, "Does this fit our wise pie?" Sometimes the answer was yes; sometimes, no.

They learned wisdom isn't squeezing more in; it's making space for what matters most.

DISCUSSION QUESTIONS

1. Which "slice" in your week needs to shrink? Which needs to grow?

2. What do we want to be true of our family time this season?

3. Where do we need to say a brave "no" so we can say a better "yes"?

FAMILY ACTIVITY: TIME PIE AND MARGIN HOUR

Draw your personal time pie. Choose one small change for the week and schedule a "margin hour" everyone protects. Put a sticky note on the fridge: "What will bring rest or connection in our hour?" Evaluate at week's end and thank God for the time you reclaimed.

PRAYER

Lord, teach us to number our days. Give us wisdom to use time well, to make space for You and each other. In Jesus' name, Amen.

Week 40: Peacemakers

"Blessed are the peacemakers, for they shall be called sons of God." — Matthew 5:9 (ESV)

OPENING THOUGHT

Peace doesn't just happen; it's made. God calls us to step toward conflict with courage, humility, and love.

FAMILY STORY

The Morales twins, Eli and Sofia, could turn any small spark into a wildfire. One afternoon, a borrowed hoodie went missing and accusations flew. Mom called a "peace huddle." She drew three steps on a whiteboard: Pause, Pray, Pursue.

First, they paused to breathe and cool down. Second, they prayed aloud: "Jesus, be our peace." Third, they pursued resolution—each shared feelings without blame, and they looked for solutions. Turns out, the hoodie was in the car under a soccer ball. The bigger issue was respect for each other's things.

They made a plan: a shared hook by the door for borrowed items and a simple sign-out sticky note on the fridge. The next week, when another conflict popped up over who got the front seat, Eli called, "Peace huddle!" They practiced the steps, and the argument shrank from bonfire to birthday candle.

By month's end, "peacemaker" felt less like a nice word and more like a family identity.

DISCUSSION QUESTIONS

1. Which step is hardest for you—Pause, Pray, or Pursue?

2. What tools help you be a peacemaker (timers, phrases, space, compromise)?

3. Where do you need to make the first move toward peace this week?

FAMILY ACTIVITY: PEACE PLAYBOOK

Create a small poster with the three Ps and 2-3 practical tools under each (Pause: water break, count to 20. Pray: one-sentence prayer, hold hands. Pursue: "I feel" statements, brainstorm solutions). Hang it where conflicts arise most. Celebrate peacemaking with a "peace high-five" when someone uses the playbook.

PRAYER

Prince of Peace, make us peacemakers. Help us pause, pray, and pursue reconciliation with humility and love. In Your name, Amen.

Week 41: Compassion in Action

"Rejoice with those who rejoice, weep with those who weep." — Romans 12:15 (ESV)

OPENING THOUGHT

Compassion feels and does. It celebrates others' joys and enters their pain with presence, prayer, and practical help.

FAMILY STORY

When Mrs. Alvarez across the street lost her husband, the neighborhood grew quiet. The Patel family had waved at her for years but hadn't talked much. Eleven-year-old Arjun asked, "What can we do?" Dad said, "Start with presence."

They wrote a simple card: "We're so sorry. We're here." They brought soup and sat on the porch while Mrs. Alvarez told stories—how her husband loved cheesy jokes and always over-watered the fern. They laughed and cried together.

Over the next month, the Patels organized a lawn crew schedule and invited neighbors to sign up. Arjun drew a small picture for her fridge each week—tiny bright windows of color. On a hard Sunday, Mrs. Alvarez came to church with them.

During the final hymn, she squeezed Mom's hand and whispered, "Thank you for not leaving me alone."

Compassion didn't fix grief. It made sure grief didn't have to walk alone. And it taught the Patels to celebrate and to weep—together.

DISCUSSION QUESTIONS

1. Who in our circle is rejoicing? Who is weeping? How can we join them?

2. What makes it hard to show up for people in pain?

3. What practical help can we offer someone this week?

FAMILY ACTIVITY: COMPASSION CALENDAR

Draw a two-week calendar. Fill it with small acts: write a card, deliver a snack, send a text, mow a lawn, pray a specific Scripture. Assign names to days. At the end, reflect on what you learned about God's heart and your neighbors' stories.

PRAYER

Father of mercies, teach us to rejoice and to weep with others. Fill our hearts with Your compassion and our hands with practical love. In Jesus' name, Amen.

Week 42: Your Gifts, God's Glory

"As each has received a gift, use it to serve one another, as good stewards of God's varied grace."
— 1 Peter 4:10 (ESV)

OPENING THOUGHT

God gives different gifts on purpose. We don't compare; we contribute. When everyone brings their part, the body of Christ thrives.

FAMILY STORY

At the community center talent night, the Kim family signed up together. Noah juggled. Grace played violin. Mom baked lemon bars. Dad... wasn't sure. "I don't have a talent," he joked. Grace raised an eyebrow. "You fix everything."

They created a "talent booth" instead of a stage act. While Grace played soft music and Noah juggled outside to draw a crowd, Dad repaired loose table legs and squeaky doors. Mom handed out lemon bars with a sign: "Sweet treats and squeak fixes—free!"

People lined up with wobbly chairs and big smiles. A shy boy asked Noah to teach him a simple juggling trick. Grace helped an older neighbor tune his old guitar. Dad showed two teens how to use a screwdriver properly. The center director said, "This is my favorite 'act' of the night."

On the drive home, Dad said, "I guess gifts can look like lemon bars and screwdrivers." The kids laughed. They learned that every grace—seen and unseen—matters when used in love.

DISCUSSION QUESTIONS

1. What gifts do you see in each of us? Speak them out loud.

2. Where can your gifts serve someone this week?

3. What "unseen" gifts might God be inviting you to offer?

FAMILY ACTIVITY: GIFT SWAP SERVE

List each person's gifts (art, listening, fixing, baking, organizing). Pair up and plan one small service using the other person's gift—teach, assist, or spotlight it to bless someone else. Share photos or notes about how it went and what you learned from one another.

PRAYER

Giver of grace, thank You for our varied gifts. Help us use them to serve others and point to Your glory. In Jesus' name, Amen.

Week 43: Falling Forward

"for the righteous falls seven times and rises again," — Proverbs 24:16 (ESV)

OPENING THOUGHT

Failure isn't final when God is faithful. In Christ, we learn, repent, and rise—wiser and humbler than before.

FAMILY STORY

Coach Rivera posted the track meet results. Eli hadn't just missed first; he'd false-started and got disqualified. He stuffed his spikes into his bag and planned to avoid everyone. On the way out, Coach called him back. "You've got two choices: hide from this or learn from it."

At home, Eli sulked until Grandpa stopped by. "When I built cabinets," Grandpa said, "I ruined more boards than I'd like to admit. I learned to measure twice, cut once—and when I messed up, I made a smaller shelf." He grinned. "Falling forward."

Eli watched videos on starting technique and practiced with a rubber band to feel pressure without jumping. At the next meet, he finished third. Not first, but clean. As he packed up, he saw a teammate crying after a dropped baton. Eli sat beside him and said, "I know the feeling. Want to practice together this week?"

Failure had cracked Eli's pride and opened space for growth and empathy. Falling forward looked like getting up—and helping someone else up, too.

DISCUSSION QUESTIONS

1. Where have you stumbled recently? What did you learn?

2. What does "falling forward" look like in school, work, sports, or relationships?

3. How can we create a home where it's safe to try, fail, and grow?

FAMILY ACTIVITY: "MUSEUM OF OOPS"

Set up a shelf or wall with ticketed "exhibits" of past flops: a burned cookie, a bent nail, a funny photo, a story card. Under each, write what you learned and how you "rose again." Visit the museum together and thank God for growth through the "oops."

PRAYER

God, thank You that failure doesn't define us—Your grace does. Help us repent quickly, learn humbly, and rise again. In Jesus' name, Amen.

Week 44: Celebrate God's Goodness

"This is the day that the LORD has made; let us rejoice and be glad in it." — Psalm 118:24 (ESV)

OPENING THOUGHT

Celebration isn't shallow; it's spiritual. We mark God's goodness with joy—big and small—because gratitude grows when we celebrate together.

FAMILY STORY

When the Hernandez family finished paying off a lingering medical bill, they decided to throw a "God is faithful" party. Not fancy—just chili, cornbread, and a banner the kids made with markers and glitter. They invited neighbors who had prayed, a nurse who had cared for them, and the grandparents who'd watched the kids during appointments.

Before eating, they shared "stones of remembrance"—small river rocks with words like "Provision," "Help," "Patience." Each person told a short story connected to a stone and placed it in a glass jar. Laughter and a few tears mingled in the room. After dinner, they sang one simple worship chorus with a guitar that was slightly out of tune and perfectly joyful.

The next day, the jar sat on the mantel, catching sunlight. When new challenges came, the family would point to it and say, "Remember!" Celebration didn't deny future problems; it strengthened their memory of God's goodness so they could face the next hill with faith.

DISCUSSION QUESTIONS

1. What do we have to celebrate right now—answered prayer, growth, provision?

2. How does celebrating together strengthen our faith?

3. What "stones of remembrance" can we add to our story?

FAMILY ACTIVITY: REMEMBRANCE JAR PARTY

Find a clear jar and smooth stones (or paper circles). Write a word or short phrase on each that marks God's goodness. Host a simple "celebrate" dinner—invite a friend or two who played a role. Share the stories behind the stones. Keep the jar visible and add to it throughout the year.

Safety note: If very young children are present, supervise closely when using small stones (choking hazard). Consider using larger paper "stones" instead.

PRAYER

Joyful God, thank You for the gifts of today. Teach us to celebrate Your goodness and remember Your faithfulness. In Jesus' name, Amen.

Week 45: Faith at Home

"And these words that I command you today shall be on your heart. You shall teach them diligently to your children... when you sit in your house, and when you walk by the way, and when you lie down, and when you rise." — Deuteronomy 6:6-7 (ESV)

OPENING THOUGHT

Faith grows best in everyday moments—meals, drives, bedtimes, and morning routines. We don't need perfection; we need presence and simple practices.

FAMILY STORY

The O'Neals were busy, like most families. One night, Dad said, "What if we build tiny habits that stack on what we already do?" They brainstormed "when you sit, walk, lie down, rise."

They added a one-sentence blessing before dinner—rotating who speaks it. On the drive to school, Mom started a "verse of the week" challenge with a sticky note on the dashboard. At bedtime, each person shared a high, a low, and a "God sighting." In the morning, they tried "first word to God"—a quick prayer before phones or news.

At first, they forgot sometimes. They laughed and tried again. Over weeks, the habits became rhythms. The house felt more anchored. When a hard day came, the lines they'd memorized rose to the surface. When a good day came, gratitude had a well-worn path to walk.

Faith at home wasn't a program; it was a pattern—small threads woven into ordinary life, strong enough to hold.

DISCUSSION QUESTIONS

1. Which simple faith practice could we add to a daily moment we already have?

2. What helps make Scripture and prayer feel natural at home, not forced?

3. How can we share leadership so everyone participates?

FAMILY ACTIVITY: RHYTHM BUILDER

Choose four anchor moments (rise, sit/eat, walk/drive, lie down). For each, design a 1–2 minute practice: blessing, memory verse, prayer, or thankfulness. Write them on a card posted near that spot (fridge, car, bedside). Review in two weeks and adjust. Celebrate with a "Rhythm Night" dessert.

PRAYER

Lord, plant Your Word in our home. Help us teach and live Your truth in simple, faithful ways every day. In Jesus' name, Amen.

Week 46: Clean Hearts, Clear Joy

"If we confess our sins, he is faithful and just to forgive us our sins and to cleanse us from all unrighteousness." — 1 John 1:9 (ESV)

OPENING THOUGHT

Sin is like sticky mud—it clings, hides, and weighs us down. Confession isn't about wallowing; it's about walking into the light and letting God wash us clean. Clean hearts make room for clear joy.

FAMILY STORY

Saturday morning chores were buzzing along when a crash echoed from the living room. The Harper family stopped. On the floor lay Grandma's blue vase in five jagged pieces. Ten-year-old Zoe stood nearby, cheeks pale. "The cat did it," she blurted.

All day, the house felt heavy. At dinner, Dad read 1 John 1:9. He talked about how confession is an invitation, not a trap. Tears pricked Zoe's eyes. "It wasn't the cat," she whispered. "I was practicing soccer kicks inside. I'm sorry."

Silence held for a beat. Then Mom exhaled gently. "Thank you for telling the truth." Dad nodded. "We forgive you. There'll be a consequence—no indoor ball for a month and you'll help pay to repair or replace the vase—but we want your heart clean more than a vase perfect."

Zoe's shoulders relaxed. That night, she asked Grandma on video chat to forgive her. Grandma smiled kindly. "Sweetheart,

I forgive you. And I still want to see those soccer skills—outside." They all laughed.

On Sunday, the family tried a Kintsugi-style repair with gold-colored glue. The cracks didn't disappear; they gleamed. Zoe touched the rim softly. "It's different," she said, "but still beautiful." Mom hugged her. "So are forgiven hearts."

DISCUSSION QUESTIONS

1. Why is it hard to confess when we've messed up?

2. What's the difference between feeling guilty and receiving forgiveness?

3. How can we make our home a safe place for honest confession and real restoration?

FAMILY ACTIVITY: LIGHT AND LIST

Dim the lights and light a candle. Give each person a small card to privately write one thing to confess to God. Read 1 John 1:9, then silently pray and tear the card. Turn on the lights and pass around a bowl of warm water and a towel—each person dips fingers in, remembering God's cleansing. If needed, make amends with one another afterward.

Safety note: If using candles, opt for LED/battery candles with young children. Supervise the warm water bowl and keep towels handy to prevent spills. You can also use a small damp washcloth instead of a bowl.

PRAYER

Faithful Father, thank You for forgiving and cleansing us. Give us courage to live in the light, to confess quickly, and to restore gently. In Jesus' name, Amen.

Week 47: The Helper Is With Us

"But the Helper, the Holy Spirit, whom the Father will send in my name, he will teach you all things and bring to your remembrance all that I have said to you." — John 14:26 (ESV)

OPENING THOUGHT

We're not alone in following Jesus. The Holy Spirit teaches, reminds, guides, and comforts—our Helper in homework, hard talks, and heart change. Learning to listen to Him is a lifelong adventure.

FAMILY STORY

The Thompsons had a busy Tuesday: spelling bee, parent meeting, and a conversation with a neighbor who'd been hurt by a misunderstanding. "Let's invite the Helper," Mom said at breakfast. They asked the Holy Spirit to guide their words and thoughts.

At school, Maya stood backstage for the spelling bee with sweaty hands. The word "chrysalis" landed in her ears and her mind blanked. She breathed, "Help." Slowly, the letters rose like stepping-stones—c-h-r-y-s-a-l-i-s. Ding! Correct. She smiled, knowing the Helper's calm had steadied her more than any list.

That evening, Dad walked across the street to talk with Mr. Gray about the fence line. He had rehearsed a speech, but as Mr. Gray opened the door with tired eyes, something shifted. Dad felt a nudge: listen first. "How are you?" he asked. The story spilled out—job stress, a sick sister, a frazzled week. The fence issue turned into a plan they worked on together Saturday morning.

Later, Maya remembered the verse: the Holy Spirit teaches and reminds. He reminded her of the spelling, yes—but he also reminded Dad to love a neighbor. The Helper's work wasn't loud; it was faithful, practical, and present.

DISCUSSION QUESTIONS

1. When have you sensed the Holy Spirit helping, reminding, or guiding you?

2. What makes it hard to notice His nudges in daily life?

3. How can we practice asking, listening, and obeying quickly this week?

FAMILY ACTIVITY: THREE-WORD PRAYERS

Throughout the day, practice three-word prayers that invite the Spirit: "Lead me, Lord," "Teach my heart," "Give me wisdom," "Help me listen." Write a few on sticky notes around the house. Share one moment each evening when you sensed an answer.

PRAYER

Holy Spirit, thank You for being our Helper. Train our ears to hear You and our hearts to obey You with joy. In Jesus' name, Amen.

Week 48: Contentment in Every Season

*"But godliness with contentment is great gain," —
1 Timothy 6:6 (ESV)*

OPENING THOUGHT

Contentment isn't settling for less; it's resting in God's enough. When we loosen our grip on more, our hands open to gratitude and generosity.

FAMILY STORY

New sneakers dropped at the mall, and the buzz at school was loud. Jonah's pair still fit fine but didn't glow, bounce, or connect to an app. "Everyone has them," he moaned. Meanwhile, Mom scrolled used car listings, sighing over models they couldn't afford. Discontentment was catching.

At dinner, Dad suggested a "contentment week." Not a ban on buying—just a practice of noticing "enough." Each person named three things they appreciated already. Jonah looked skeptical, but he wrote: "shoes without holes," "grandpa's jokes," "mac and cheese."

They taped 1 Timothy 6:6 on the fridge and made a chart: gratitude, generosity, and goals. Gratitude for what they had. Generosity with something to share. Goals for wise saving—not to worship a purchase, but to steward well. Jonah decided to clean and relace his sneakers and sell an old game to fund a small gift for the backpack drive. Mom adjusted her car expectations and found a reliable, older model that fit the budget—no extra bells, but peace.

By week's end, their house felt lighter. The new sneakers at school still looked cool, but Jonah noticed the kid wearing them didn't seem happier. Jonah jogged home, glanced at his chart, and wrote one more gratitude: "Contentment: great gain."

DISCUSSION QUESTIONS

1. Where do you feel the tug for "more" right now?

2. What helps you practice contentment without pretending desires don't exist?

3. How can gratitude, generosity, and goals work together in our family?

FAMILY ACTIVITY: THE ENOUGH EXPERIMENT

For seven days, choose one category (clothes, snacks, entertainment) and practice "enough." Clean, repair, or repurpose what you have. Keep a visible gratitude list. Set aside a small amount to give. At week's end, share how it felt and what you learned about God's provision.

PRAYER

Provider God, teach us contentment. Fill our hearts with gratitude and free our hands for generosity. In Jesus' name, Amen.

Week 49: Outdo One Another in Honor

"Love one another with brotherly affection. Outdo one another in showing honor." — Romans 12:10 (ESV)

OPENING THOUGHT

Honor is love with manners and intention. It notices, thanks, and lifts others up—especially the people we see every day.

FAMILY STORY

Siblings Parker and Mia could turn compliments into competitions—and not the good kind. If Parker got praise for his science fair model, Mia rolled her eyes. If Mia nailed a piano piece, Parker muttered, "Big deal." The house felt like a scoreboard with no winners.

One evening, Mom read Romans 12:10 and proposed an "Honor Challenge." For one week, they'd try to outdo one another in showing honor. Not flattery—real, specific encouragement and acts of respect.

Day one, Parker left a sticky note on the piano: "Your timing on the bridge sounded pro." Mia blinked. That afternoon, she cleaned up the Lego explosion in the living room without being asked and told Parker, "Your designs are getting smoother." Parker felt something tighten, then soften. Honor wasn't weakness; it was strength turned outward.

By day four, Dad caught the bug, too. He thanked Mom for managing a complicated calendar and took the car for an oil change without being asked. Mom honored Grandma by calling and asking for her famous soup recipe, then crediting her at dinner.

By week's end, the scoreboard was covered in sticky notes and small services. Parker admitted, "Outdoing each other in honor is the only competition where everybody wins."

DISCUSSION QUESTIONS

1. What does honor look like at home—words, tone, actions?

2. Who is someone we often overlook that we can honor this week?

3. How does honoring others change our hearts?

FAMILY ACTIVITY: HONOR WALL

Create a wall or door space for "honor notes." Write specific encouragements and appreciations—name the effort, not just the result. Add simple acts of honor to a jar (let someone go first, do their chore, ask about their day). Draw one daily. Review together on the weekend and give thanks.

PRAYER

Lord, teach us to outdo one another in showing honor. Make our home a place where encouragement flows and respect grows. In Jesus' name, Amen.

Week 50: Hiding God's Word in Our Hearts

"I have stored up your word in my heart, that I might not sin against you." — Psalm 119:11 (ESV)

OPENING THOUGHT

Memorizing Scripture isn't just for quizzers; it's fuel for faith. God's Word in our hearts becomes strength in temptation, comfort in trouble, and wisdom on the go.

FAMILY STORY

On Tuesday, Ava felt the familiar pull to join in when classmates gossiped. The words were juicy, the circle tight. Then she heard a quiet echo in her mind: "Let no corrupting talk come out of your mouths..." She'd memorized Ephesians 4:29 last month with her cousin. She changed the subject—awkward, but freeing.

That night, Dad confessed feeling anxious before a presentation. He whispered Psalm 56:3 on repeat: "When I am afraid, I put my trust in you." His heart slowed. Mom shared how Psalm 23 steadied her during a long wait at the doctor's office.

Their family decided to build a "verse pantry." They picked four short verses for the month and posted them by the sink, in the car, and near beds. They made a game of it—call-and-response at dinner, verse charades, and a "memory path" where each step on the stairs matched a word. Scripture seeped in through smiles and stumbles.

By month's end, verses surfaced naturally—during sibling squabbles, stressful emails, and late-night worries. God's Word didn't just sit on pages; it lived in their hearts, ready when they needed it most.

DISCUSSION QUESTIONS

1. What situations this week need a "ready verse" for strength or wisdom?

2. What helps you memorize best—songs, motions, writing, or repetition?

3. How can we cheer each other on without making it feel like pressure?

FAMILY ACTIVITY: VERSE PANTRY PLAN

Pick four short verses (one per week). Write them on cards and place them in three spots: sink, car, bedside. Choose a practice: say it at meals, sing it with a simple tune, or do motions. At week's end, share one moment when the verse helped in real life.

PRAYER

God, plant Your Word deep in us. Help us store it in our hearts so we can live wisely, love well, and stand strong. In Jesus' name, Amen.

Week 51: Carry Each Other

"Bear one another's burdens, and so fulfill the law
of Christ." — Galatians 6:2 (ESV)

OPENING THOUGHT

We're not meant to shoulder life alone. In the body of Christ,
we share loads—practical, emotional, and spiritual—so no one
buckles under the weight.

FAMILY STORY

When Mrs. Green's husband had surgery, the church set up
a meal train. The Jacksons signed up for Tuesday. Ten-year-
old Leo wrote a card; Mom made chicken soup; Dad offered
to drive Mrs. Green to a follow-up appointment. Simple. But
when they delivered the food, they discovered the fridge was
broken.

Dad called a friend who repairs appliances. Leo offered to
store some items in their fridge. Mom set up a cooler with ice.
They prayed with Mrs. Green in her kitchen while the repair
was scheduled. On Thursday, the appliance friend fixed it at a
discount. Mrs. Green cried, not from the bill, but from relief.

That week, Leo told his class about "burden-carrying." A classmate quietly said his family needed help with rides while his
mom worked late. The Jacksons added him to their carpool.
The circle widened.

By Sunday, the Jacksons were tired—but a good tired, the kind
that follows love. They realized burden-bearing wasn't a one-

time task; it was a lifestyle that fulfilled the law of Christ: love your neighbor.

DISCUSSION QUESTIONS

1. What burdens are we carrying that we need help with?

2. Who around us needs shoulder-to-shoulder help this week?

3. What keeps us from asking for or offering help, and how can we move past it?

FAMILY ACTIVITY: BURDEN BOARD

On a small board, list family burdens (projects, appointments, worries) and community burdens (neighbors, friends). Assign helpers for each—who prays, who drives, who cooks, who checks in. Review midweek and swap roles as needed. Celebrate small wins with a "burden high-five."

PRAYER

Jesus, You carried our greatest burden at the cross. Make us humble enough to ask for help and generous enough to give it. Teach us to love like You. Amen.

Week 52: Love God, Love People

"You shall love the Lord your God with all your heart and with all your soul and with all your mind... And a second is like it: You shall love your neighbor as yourself." — Matthew 22:37-39 (ESV)

OPENING THOUGHT

This is the big picture: love God fully and love people faithfully. Every habit we've practiced points here. As we finish this year, we begin again—rooted in love.

FAMILY STORY

The Nguyen family decided to end their devotional year with a "Love God, Love People" day. In the morning, they took a quiet walk by the river, reading Matthew 22 and thanking God for the year's small transformations—less yelling, more listening; less hurry, more presence. They wrote prayers of gratitude on index cards and tied them to a small tree in the yard with ribbon.

In the afternoon, they hosted a simple block party—hot dogs, lemonade, a chalk obstacle course, and a "Take What You Need" table with extra school supplies and canned goods. Mr. Dean brought roses from his garden for a bouquet station. The kids made a "Prayer Corner" with crayons where people could write requests. Neighbors swapped stories, laughter rose, and someone asked, "Why do you all do this?" Mom smiled. "Because God loves us, and we love our neighbors."

As the sun set, they gathered to pray through the cards from the Prayer Corner. Some needs were heavy, some hopeful. The family realized loving God with all their heart naturally spilled into loving people with open hands. The year ended not with a period but with a comma—more love ahead.

DISCUSSION QUESTIONS

1. Looking back, where have we seen God grow love in our family this year?

2. What rhythms do we want to carry into the next season?

3. Who is one neighbor we can love intentionally this month?

FAMILY ACTIVITY: LOVE RULES RULE

Create a simple two-rule poster: 1) Love God—heart, soul, mind. 2) Love people—as yourself. Under each, list three practical ways your family will live them out this month (worship, Scripture, prayer; hospitality, service, encouragement). Place it where you'll see it daily and review weekly.

PRAYER

Lord, thank You for this year of growing with You. Help us keep the main thing the main thing: loving You with everything and loving our neighbors well. Lead us by Your Spirit into another year of grace. In Jesus' name, Amen.

Discover More Books

Start each day with purpose, peace, and spiritual renewal.

Whether you're guiding teens in faith or growing closer as a family—this devotional series meets you right where you are.

Collect the Whole Series

Devotional for Parents and Kids

Devotional for Teen Girls

Devotional for Teen Boys

Available at major online bookstores

Each book is a spiritual companion. Together, they form a complete journey—personal, relational, and transformative.

Don't wait—bring home the full devotional set and let every day draw you closer to faith, love, and lasting renewal.